RUNAWAY OR TAKEN?

The Mystery of Phoenix Coldon

Linda Davidson

For Phoenix— and for every family who keeps the candle lit when the world grows quiet.

"For we walk by faith, not by sight." — *2 Corinthians 5:7*

— 2 CORINTHIANS 5:7

PREFACE

I did not meet Phoenix Coldon. I met the absence she left behind —an idling car on Old Jamestown Road, a purse and glasses on the passenger seat, a family waiting at a window that still glows with a single candle each December. This book begins there, not because a mystery is most dramatic at its first unanswerable moment, but because the first hours are where systems either protect a life—or quietly lose it.

Runaway or Taken? is narrative nonfiction built from public records, broadcast transcripts, interviews, advocacy reports, and the words of those who have refused to let Phoenix's name fade. Where accounts conflict or the record is thin, I say so. Where a theory is only that, I label it. There are no composite characters here, no invented dialogue, no "tidying up" of time. A missing person case is not a story to be solved; it is a life to be honored while the facts are pursued with patience.

Two forces shape these pages. The first is love—the stubborn, organizing love of Goldia and Lawrence Coldon. In their living room, faith is not sentiment; it is logistics: call logs, binders, maps, a phone that stays charged overnight. The second is silence—the procedural gaps, jurisdictional drift, and media indifference that too often decide whose absence becomes urgent and whose is filed under "wait and see." Phoenix's case exposes that silence without exploiting her or anyone who remains living inside it.

You will not find verdicts here. You will find timelines carefully reconciled; what we know and what we don't separated by clear lines; and the dignity of a young woman protected when speculation runs ahead of evidence. When a choice had to be made between drama and care, I chose care. When sources disagreed, I let the most conservative reading prevail. When the family's privacy would be compromised by detail, I withheld it unless it materially changed the reader's understanding of risk, process, or responsibility.

This book also asks a wider question: who gets found? The disparity in attention surrounding missing persons is not abstract here; it is practical and measurable. It shows up in the hours before a case is treated as urgent, in the decision to tow a vehicle before it is fully processed, in which photos make the evening news and which ones don't. Phoenix's story lives at the intersection of those decisions. To tell it faithfully is to reckon with them.

Readers of true crime bring different hungers to the page—answers, justice, catharsis. I can offer only the first two in partial forms, and the third not at all. What I can offer is accuracy without spectacle; empathy without intrusion; and clear pages you can hand to someone who needs to understand what happened, what didn't, and why the difference matters. If you arrive at the final chapter with fewer certainties than you expected, that is not failure; it is fidelity to a case that remains open, to a family that is still searching, and to a woman whose life cannot be reduced to a single afternoon.

A word about harm. Public attention can help and it can wound. Crowds can surface tips and they can misidentify neighbors. This manuscript avoids naming uncharged individuals, declines to print unverified addresses, and does not amplify rumors that would outlive their utility. When I describe investigative errors, I do so to improve future response, not to score points against people who were overworked, undertrained, or answering calls in good faith inside imperfect systems. Accountability and charity can occupy the same sentence.

If you are here for a map, you will get one—of minutes and miles, calls and gaps, the narrow corridor between "ran away" and "was taken" that swallows so many women in America. If you are here for meaning, you will find it in small places: a mother's steady voice at a vigil, a father visiting the shoulder where the world went quiet, neighbors who keep showing up when cameras do not. If you are here for a task, you will find that too: learn the early steps that save time, share a flyer responsibly, donate to groups that center the missing without exploiting them, and say Phoenix's name with the gravity it deserves.

The candle in the Coldons' window is not a prop. It is instruction. It says keep watch. It says do not look away. It says a life is not a headline, and a headline is not an ending. May these pages keep that light steady—and may they shorten, even by a little, the distance between what happened and what we are finally able to say aloud.

LEGAL & ETHICS NOTE

This book concerns a missing-person case involving living individuals. Care has been taken to avoid speculation, protect privacy, and distinguish confirmed facts from theory. Names of private persons are limited or anonymized where appropriate. Readers should consult official updates for developments that may postdate this edition.

Content Note

This book includes references to disappearance, possible violence, and ongoing trauma. Reader discretion is advised.

AUTHOR'S NOTE TO THE READER

I wrote this book in the tension between urgency and care. When sources conflicted, I chose patience; when facts were missing, I said so. May these pages honor a daughter, equip other families, and widen the circle of people who refuse to look away.

— **Linda Davidson**

PERMISSIONS & CREDITS

Quotations from broadcasts, interviews, and public statements are used under fair use for news, commentary, and scholarship. Every effort has been made to trace rights holders; contact the publisher with corrections for future editions.

DISCLAIMER

This is a work of narrative nonfiction. Events have been reconstructed from publicly available records, interviews, contemporaneous reporting, and advocacy materials. Where the record is incomplete or accounts conflict, uncertainty is identified and the most conservative reading prevails. No dialogue is invented, and speculation is labeled as such.

All persons named or described as suspects, persons of interest, or otherwise connected to any investigation are presumed innocent unless and until proven guilty in a court of law. Allegations remain allegations.

Out of respect for privacy and safety, some identifying details of private individuals have been limited or omitted when doing so does not materially affect the reader's understanding. Any resemblance to living persons in anonymized examples is coincidental and unintentional.

Procedures, laws, and case statuses may have changed after the time of writing. Readers should consult official sources for the most current information. This book is not legal, medical, or investigative advice.

Content note: The text references disappearance, potential violence, and ongoing trauma. Reader discretion is advised.

PROLOGUE

— The Car on Old Jamestown Road

The air that afternoon was still enough to make the trees look like they were holding their breath. It was December 18, 2011, a Sunday in North County, St. Louis. The temperature hovered in the forties—gray skies, a thin winter sun—and traffic was light along Old Jamestown Road, a stretch of pavement that wound through open lots and patches of trees. Just before dusk, a call came in to the police: a black 1998 Chevy Blazer was sitting oddly at the side of the road, engine still running, driver's door open.

When the first officer arrived, he found the vehicle idling quietly. The radio hummed. The key was still in the ignition. On the passenger seat lay a purse and glasses. Inside the cup holder was a half-empty drink, condensation streaking the plastic. There were no signs of struggle—no skid marks, no broken glass, no blood. It was as if the driver had simply stepped out and vanished into thin air.

The license plate traced the car back to a young woman named **Phoenix Coldon**. Twenty-three years old. College student. Musician. Devout Christian. A former fencing champion who could quote scripture and out-argue anyone in debate club. Her parents, Goldia and Lawrence Coldon, hadn't even realized she was missing. They thought she was out running errands or heading to church rehearsal, the way she often did on Sundays. By the time they learned the car had been towed, nearly twelve hours had passed.

It was the first crack in a mystery that would widen until it swallowed a family's peace, a city's conscience, and eventually, the trust of everyone who tried to make sense of it.

When investigators walked through the details, nothing fit neatly. Phoenix's purse contained her driver's license and keys—things no one leaves behind voluntarily. Her phone was missing, but calls had stopped abruptly that afternoon. There were no charges on her credit card, no withdrawals from her bank. Friends described her as private but grounded; no one believed she had simply run away. Yet the evidence of foul play was thin—no witnesses, no struggle, no body.

As hours became days, speculation took root. Some whispered that Phoenix might have left on her own—escaping pressure from college, church, or home. Others feared something darker: an abduction, a trafficking ring, a random act of violence that went unnoticed in a city numb to crime.

The case file grew but not the leads. Detectives came and went. Jurisdiction lines blurred between city and county police. Calls went unanswered. The Coldons started their own search—handing out flyers, knocking on doors, praying out loud when words no longer sufficed. Each night, Goldia lit a candle by the front window, convinced her daughter would see it if she found her way home.

What haunted them most was the silence—the way Phoenix's name barely crossed newscasts, the absence of urgency in headlines that burned for others but dimmed for her. Her parents wondered if their daughter's disappearance would have drawn more attention if she had looked different, lived elsewhere, been someone else's child.

Years later, people still argue about what happened on Old Jamestown Road. Some think Phoenix fled to start over, her own rebirth echoing the meaning of her name. Others believe she was taken—by someone she trusted, by a stranger who saw opportunity, or by a system too slow to see her as a priority.

But the truth remains stranded somewhere between those two possibilities—**Runaway or Taken**—like that car idling at the side of the road, the air growing colder, the daylight fading, and a mother's prayer stretching into another sleepless night.

CHAPTER 1 THE GIRL NAMED PHOENIX

Phoenix Lucille Coldon—a name that carried fire and flight, as if her parents had somehow known she'd live a life that would burn bright and leave behind questions no one could quite extinguish.

Born in St. Louis, Missouri, on May 23, 1988, Phoenix grew up in a house that echoed with gospel hymns and the steady rhythm of structure. Her father, **Lawrence Coldon**, was a soft-spoken man who worked in security and believed in boundaries—faith, education, hard work. Her mother, **Goldia**, was a powerhouse of conviction and discipline. The Coldons were the kind of family that prayed together before dinner, kept curfews, and valued church as much as grades. Phoenix was their only child, their "miracle baby," as Goldia often said.

From an early age, Phoenix stood out—not just for her intelligence, but for her curiosity about everything. She learned piano by ear before she could read sheet music. She debated teachers on philosophy before she turned twelve. When other kids stayed home, she fenced—an uncommon sport in North County, especially for a Black girl in a suburban Catholic school uniform.

She excelled at it too, earning medals and praise that made her both proud and uncomfortable. Phoenix wasn't looking for attention; she was looking for meaning.

At church, she played with the youth worship team, singing harmonies that carried through the sanctuary with soulful precision. She led Bible studies, volunteered, and read voraciously —C.S. Lewis, Maya Angelou, and law textbooks she wasn't required to read. Her parents often called her "wise beyond her years." But wisdom didn't protect her from the quiet, restless questions that began to form in her early twenties.

The Restless Years

By 2011, Phoenix was twenty-three and living at home again after attending the University of Missouri–St. Louis. Like many young adults, she was caught between dependence and independence— between the expectations of faith and the pull of freedom. Friends said she seemed different in those final months—more private, more guarded, like someone who had too many tabs open in her mind.

She had stopped attending church as regularly as before. Some said she was frustrated with her parents' strictness. Others thought she was exploring who she was beyond the labels of "the church girl" and "the prodigy." There were rumors of a boyfriend her parents didn't approve of, whispers of arguments about her future, and subtle changes in her demeanor.

Still, to those who knew her best, she remained the same Phoenix —kind, sharp, and sincere, even when she felt misunderstood. She spoke often about wanting to travel, to do something meaningful, to leave behind the smallness of routine and expectations. Her mother later admitted that she sometimes worried Phoenix was slipping into something she couldn't quite name—something spiritual, emotional, or maybe both.

The Day She Disappeared

Sunday, December 18, 2011, began like any other. Phoenix attended church with her parents that morning. The service ran long, and afterward, they returned home for lunch. Goldia remembered Phoenix sitting on the couch, flipping through her phone, quiet but not withdrawn. Around 2 p.m., Phoenix stepped outside. She said nothing about where she was going. She didn't take a coat. She wore gray sweatpants, a hoodie, tennis shoes, and her hair pulled back—comfortable, ordinary.

An hour passed. Then two.

When she hadn't returned by nightfall, her parents began to worry. Phoenix was usually punctual, even when she needed space. Calls to her cell went straight to voicemail. Goldia tried to convince herself her daughter was fine—out with friends, delayed somewhere safe. But when midnight came and there was still no word, instinct told her something was wrong.

The next morning, the phone rang. It was the police.

Phoenix's 1998 Chevy Blazer had been found abandoned on Old Jamestown Road—engine still running.

Goldia's world went silent. Lawrence grabbed his keys. They drove in disbelief to the impound lot, where the black SUV sat behind a chain-link fence, dusted with cold air and questions. Inside were Phoenix's glasses and purse, just as they had been left. Her seatbelt was unbuckled. The radio was still tuned to her favorite Christian station. To her parents, it felt like she'd just stepped out for a moment and was still coming back. But she never did.

The Echo of a Name

In the days that followed, the Coldons' house filled with people—

family, church members, volunteers, reporters, and prayer groups. Flyers covered telephone poles and bulletin boards. Local news stations ran brief clips about a "missing young woman," but the coverage faded quickly, replaced by louder stories, other headlines.

Her parents refused to give up. They organized search teams, combed wooded areas, and pleaded for anyone with information to come forward. Lawrence, a quiet man by nature, found himself on camera, begging for help. Goldia, fiery and articulate, became the face of their fight for attention—calling newsrooms, challenging officials, and asking the question no parent should ever have to ask: *Why isn't my daughter's story worth airtime?*

They clung to their faith, to each other, and to the conviction that the truth would eventually rise—like their daughter's name promised.

But as the days stretched into months, and the months into years, hope had to learn how to coexist with doubt. Some said Phoenix had chosen to disappear, starting a new life somewhere far away. Others whispered she'd been taken, pulled into the dark network of human trafficking that preyed on young women near the highways of the Midwest.

Each theory carried its own pain, its own kind of loss. But for Goldia and Lawrence, there was only one truth worth holding on to:

Phoenix was out there somewhere—and they were not going to stop until they found her.

CHAPTER 2 VANISHED AT NOON

The last hours before Phoenix disappeared were unremarkable in every visible way. There were no strange phone calls, no cries for help, no signs of fear or panic. That was part of what made the case so chilling—how ordinary the day seemed until, suddenly, it wasn't.

It was a quiet Sunday in December. The Coldon family attended their usual church service at the **St. Louis Church of Christ**, sitting together in their familiar pew. The pastor spoke about patience and trust—how faith often demands waiting for what we can't see. It was a sermon that would take on unbearable meaning for her parents later that night.

Afterward, they drove home to their modest house in Spanish Lake. Goldia cooked lunch. Lawrence went out to rake leaves. Phoenix moved through the house with a calm that gave no clue to what was about to unfold. She played the piano for a few minutes, checked her phone, and talked briefly to her mother about school. She seemed preoccupied, but not troubled.

Sometime between 2:00 and 3:00 p.m., Phoenix slipped on a pair of gray sweatpants, a dark hoodie, and tennis shoes. She said she was stepping out "for a bit." She didn't say where. She didn't take her ID or her glasses. Goldia assumed she was heading to the store or visiting a friend. It was normal enough not to raise alarm.

The Drive That Should Have Ended at Home

Old Jamestown Road is a winding strip of asphalt about ten minutes from the Coldon residence. It connects suburban neighborhoods to stretches of farmland and scattered churches —a corridor between everyday life and quiet isolation. Sometime that afternoon, Phoenix drove her black 1998 Chevy Blazer down that road. What happened next remains one of the most perplexing mysteries of modern missing-person cases.

Around **5:27 p.m.**, a passing motorist noticed the SUV parked awkwardly on the shoulder—engine still running, driver's door ajar. The hazard lights weren't on, and the vehicle wasn't disabled. It looked as if the driver had stopped suddenly and stepped out mid-thought. The witness called police.

When officers arrived, they found the car empty. The keys were still in the ignition, the engine humming softly. Her purse and glasses sat on the passenger seat. Her shoes were neatly placed under the steering wheel. There were no signs of a struggle— no footprints in the mud, no discarded items nearby. It was as if Phoenix had been erased mid-sentence.

The SUV was towed to an impound lot that evening. Officers ran the plates, but because the registration listed the vehicle under her father's name, they didn't immediately connect it to a missing person. It would be almost **twelve hours** before the Coldons discovered that their daughter's car had been found—and by then, Phoenix was long gone.

The Call That Changed Everything

At dawn, the phone rang. Goldia answered, groggy but hopeful. Maybe Phoenix was calling. Instead, it was the police. A car matching their registration had been impounded overnight. "Is your daughter home?" the officer asked.

Goldia froze. "She was supposed to be," she said.

Within minutes, she and Lawrence were on their way to the impound lot. The sun was low and colorless, the city wrapped in a thin layer of frost. Goldia's heart pounded as the lot attendant led them to the vehicle. There it was—Phoenix's Blazer, behind a chain-link fence, its paint dull under the pale light.

Lawrence peered inside. He recognized his daughter's purse immediately. He saw her glasses, the half-empty drink, the key still turned in the ignition. "She wouldn't leave this," he whispered.

Something inside Goldia cracked open. A mother's intuition doesn't need forensic evidence. She knew—*something was wrong*.

The Investigation Begins—Too Late

The initial police response was procedural at best, detached at worst. Because the car had already been towed before the family reported Phoenix missing, vital evidence may have been compromised. Officers didn't treat the site as a potential crime scene. No photographs were taken of the exact position of the car before it was moved. No detailed search of the surrounding woods was conducted that evening.

When Goldia and Lawrence filed a missing-person report, they were told that Phoenix was an adult—she might have "just needed space." That phrase would echo in their heads for years.

While the Coldons organized community searches, law enforcement seemed hesitant to escalate. There was no Amber Alert. No immediate canvassing of nearby security cameras or witnesses. Days passed before the case gained any formal traction, and by then, the trail had cooled.

Unanswered Questions

If Phoenix had left voluntarily, why abandon her car mid-road? Why leave her purse, glasses, and essentials behind? If she had been forced out, how could there be no witnesses, no struggle, no tire tracks?

Investigators checked her phone records. Her last call ended around **2:20 p.m.**, not long before she left home. After that, her phone went dark. No pings, no messages, no activity.

Friends said she hadn't mentioned plans to meet anyone that day. There were rumors of a secret relationship—someone she might have been meeting in confidence—but nothing concrete.

The unanswered questions multiplied. For every theory, there was an equal and opposite contradiction.

- If she was kidnapped, why wasn't there a trace?
- If she ran away, why take nothing?
- If she meant to return, what stopped her?

The questions pressed against the silence like hands against glass —visible, but never breaking through.

The Hours That Haunt

By the time darkness fell over St. Louis that night, the Coldons' lives had split in two: *before* and *after*. Before—when Phoenix was home, safe, laughing. After—when her absence became a daily ache that refused to dull.

Goldia would replay every sound from that afternoon—the door closing, the car starting, the seconds of silence that followed. If only she had asked where Phoenix was going. If only she had looked out the window.

In her mind, the clock on that day never moved past 3:00 p.m. It was always early afternoon, the sun always low, and her daughter always just about to walk back through the door.

CHAPTER 3 THE INVESTIGATION THAT STALLED

The morning after Phoenix disappeared, the world did not stop. That was the cruelest part for her parents. The mail still came. Neighbors still waved from driveways, unaware. The city still moved with its usual rhythm — as if one missing woman was just another unnoticed absence in a place accustomed to loss.

For **Goldia and Lawrence Coldon**, time no longer moved forward. It folded in on itself, trapping them in an endless loop of questions that no one seemed willing — or equipped — to answer.

By Tuesday, two days after Phoenix vanished, they expected to hear from detectives. Instead, they found themselves dialing the precinct, repeating the same explanation to new voices. Each time, the same polite but hollow tone: *"We're looking into it."*

What they didn't realize was that their daughter's case had already been misfiled — caught in a bureaucratic tangle between **St. Louis**

County Police and **St. Louis City Police**. The car had been found on a boundary road. The jurisdiction line was a matter of yards, but it was enough to create confusion over which department had authority. For the next several weeks, critical coordination would stall as both departments quietly assumed the other was taking lead.

By the time the paperwork reached the right desk, vital days had been lost.

A Cold Response

When the Coldons finally met with investigators, they arrived armed with notes, maps, and faith. Lawrence carried a folder filled with phone records. Goldia brought a Bible and a photograph of Phoenix — smiling, confident, radiant.

What they encountered was a wall of procedural detachment.

Phoenix was twenty-three, they were told. Adults had the right to disappear. There was no evidence of foul play. Maybe she'd left to clear her head. Maybe she was with friends. Maybe she'd be back soon.

It was a script they had heard before — the quiet dismissal reserved for cases that didn't seem urgent enough, dramatic enough, or, as Goldia later put it, *"photogenic enough."*

She didn't mince words when she spoke to reporters later:

"If Phoenix had looked like somebody else's daughter, this would have been national news by now."

At first, it sounded like anger. Later, it was recognized as truth.

Lost Evidence, Lost Momentum

The car, impounded within hours of being found, had already

been returned to the Coldons before investigators realized what they had. It was washed and cleaned — not processed for fingerprints or DNA. The lot attendant had tossed Phoenix's drink, vacuumed the mats, and wiped the dashboard. Whatever traces might have existed were gone.

The Coldons drove the car back home and parked it in their driveway, staring at it as if it might somehow give up its secrets. Goldia would sit in the driver's seat sometimes, trying to feel what her daughter might have felt that afternoon — if she'd been afraid, if she'd been coerced, if she'd simply planned to come back and never could.

Forensic opportunities vanished along with the initial urgency. Surveillance footage from nearby traffic cameras was erased after its retention period expired. Witness follow-ups were delayed. The area where the SUV had been found was not re-searched until much later, long after weather and time had erased any footprints or tire marks.

Every small oversight compounded into something irreversible.

The Media That Looked Away

When Phoenix first went missing, local media gave the case minimal coverage — a few seconds on the evening news, a short column buried in the metro section.

There were no national alerts, no televised interviews, no extended features.

Goldia began calling newsrooms herself. "My daughter is missing," she'd say. "Can you please run her picture again?"

The responses were polite but brief. There were other stories, other priorities. She watched as missing-person cases involving white women from nearby towns drew extensive coverage — features, live updates, national segments. Each time she turned on the television, she felt the sting of invisibility.

It was not until the **Coldons appeared on a cable news special in 2013**, two years after Phoenix vanished, that national audiences even learned her name.

By then, the trail was ice-cold.

The Family That Refused to Stop

If the police were reluctant and the media indifferent, the Coldons became both detectives and publicists. Lawrence canvassed neighborhoods and industrial parks, handing out flyers and asking if anyone had seen the black Blazer that day. Goldia began maintaining a binder of leads, writing down every rumor, every phone call, every anonymous tip.

They drove to nearby towns, truck stops, and shelters. They met with pastors and community leaders. They even checked hospitals and morgues, unwilling to let official silence replace their own search for truth.

In church, they prayed not just for answers but for endurance. Goldia spoke often about how faith can coexist with fury — how prayer doesn't erase pain but gives it shape.

"I had to believe God knew where my baby was," she said later.

"But I also had to ask why He hadn't shown anyone else."

A Systemic Silence

As weeks turned into months, Phoenix's case became a study in institutional neglect. The **National Crime Information Center (NCIC)** didn't enter her name into the missing-person database immediately. Inter-agency communication was fragmented. Leads from social media were ignored or logged without follow-up.

Behind each oversight was a deeper question about whose stories are pursued and whose are forgotten.

Phoenix was young, educated, and ambitious — but she was also a Black woman in a country where missing women of color rarely make front-page news.

In 2016, a criminologist who studied the disparity called it "missing white woman syndrome." The Coldons didn't need a term for it. They lived it.

Every time a new case dominated headlines, Goldia felt both empathy and ache — empathy for those families, ache for her own. "I just want my daughter's name to matter," she said.

Faith in the Waiting

By the end of the first year, the official investigation had grown thin. Tips had dwindled, and media attention had faded. But in the Coldon household, the search never stopped.

Each morning, Goldia brewed coffee and prayed aloud. Lawrence checked email for any message, any clue. They built a small home office filled with maps, binders, and contact lists. They stopped marking holidays as celebrations; they became checkpoints in time.

They learned how to wait — not passively, but purposefully, believing that waiting can be an act of resistance.

Because what else is faith, when the world refuses to move?

CHAPTER 4 MEDIA SILENCE AND RACIAL BIAS

In the weeks after Phoenix disappeared, her photograph circulated quietly — a smiling young woman with soft brown eyes and a radiant face framed by natural curls. On paper, she was everything a reporter might call "a story worth telling": a church-going college student, athletic, disciplined, with dreams of law school.

But in reality, few stories like hers made it past the local news crawl.

When Goldia Coldon first watched the nightly broadcasts, she noticed the difference. Young white women who vanished under similar or even less mysterious circumstances were the center of entire news cycles — full segments with maps, time stamps, and emotional music. Reporters spoke their names with gravity and compassion.

For Phoenix, there was none of that.

Just a single thirty-second mention: *"Police are searching for a local woman last seen Sunday afternoon."*

Then the anchor smiled and moved on.

It wasn't that Phoenix's disappearance was unworthy of attention. It was that it didn't fit the mold of the stories America was conditioned to care about.

The Pattern of the Invisible

Sociologists call it *media hierarchy* — the unspoken ranking of whose suffering is deemed newsworthy.

Missing Black women rarely appear at the top of that hierarchy.

When data analyst **Natalie Wilson** of the *Black and Missing Foundation* reviewed coverage between 2011 and 2012, she found a familiar pattern: despite making up nearly **40% of all missing women in the U.S.**, Black women accounted for **less than 15%** of cases reported in national media.

The disparity was not just about bias in coverage — it was about *perception*. Who looks like a victim? Whose disappearance is viewed as a crisis, and whose is quietly treated as a choice?

Phoenix's story fell into that gap between tragedy and assumption. She was too disciplined to be dismissed as reckless, but too independent to fit the fragile, endangered archetype that the media so often valorized. Her faith, her intelligence, her quiet strength — the very traits that defined her — seemed to work against her in a system that demanded drama over depth.

Goldia's Fight for a Headline

Goldia Coldon refused to let her daughter's story fade into

that silence. She became a one-woman newsroom, cold-calling producers, emailing editors, and walking into local stations with flyers.

"If I have to tell this story myself," she said in one early interview, "then that's what I'll do."

She started writing letters — to churches, to civic groups, to politicians. She launched social media pages long before "missing-person awareness" became a trend. Her posts were raw, written late at night between exhaustion and prayer:

"Phoenix Coldon is not a statistic. She is my daughter. She has a name, a face, and a purpose. Please help us bring her home."

Occasionally, a reporter would visit the Coldon home, film a short segment, and promise to "keep the story alive." But the airwaves moved on as quickly as they arrived.

Goldia understood something that few outsiders did — that justice often begins not with police, but with persistence.

A National Awakening — Too Late

It took nearly two years for Phoenix's case to reach national television. In 2013, she was featured on an episode of *"Find Our Missing"* — a TV One series dedicated to bringing attention to missing Black Americans.

For the first time, millions heard her story. They saw her smile, her church photos, her fencing medals, her mother's trembling hands. It was both a breakthrough and a heartbreak. The exposure was powerful, but it came too late. Leads that could have mattered were years cold.

Goldia later said, "It felt like finally someone was listening — but Phoenix deserved that when it could still have made a difference."

After the broadcast, new tips surfaced — sightings, vague connections, whispers about a secret relationship, even rumors that she had been trafficked. But none of them could be verified. The case, once again, receded into the background of America's collective attention span.

The Broader Silence

Phoenix's case was not an anomaly.

In 2011 alone, **over 64,000 Black women and girls** were reported missing in the United States. Few names reached public consciousness.

Criminologists and advocates have long noted that missing Black victims are more likely to be labeled "runaways" or "voluntary absences" — terms that slow or stop early investigation efforts. Media coverage often mirrors law enforcement bias, focusing on perceived lifestyle or neighborhood rather than humanity.

In contrast, missing white women are often portrayed as innocent victims whose lives must be restored.

The difference is subtle but devastating — one invites empathy, the other apathy.

Phoenix's story exposed this inequity to those willing to look closely. Her disappearance wasn't only about what happened to one woman; it revealed how easily some lives are allowed to vanish twice — first in reality, then in public memory.

Faith as Resistance

In interviews, Goldia spoke not only about her daughter but about the larger community of families who shared her pain. She began connecting with other parents — mothers whose children had disappeared without coverage, without press conferences, without justice.

Together, they prayed, organized, and pushed for visibility. They called themselves *"faithful mothers of the unseen."*

Goldia once said,

"We may never have their platforms, but we have our voices. God gave us those for a reason."

Her voice — once trembling — grew resolute.

Each time she spoke Phoenix's name, she was defying the silence that tried to erase her.

What Her Case Exposed

By 2015, true-crime podcasts and social media advocacy began reshaping the landscape of awareness. A new generation of listeners discovered Phoenix Coldon's story — not through police updates, but through empathy-driven storytelling.

People were drawn not only to the mystery but to the *meaning*. Phoenix had become a symbol — of how systemic neglect could hide beneath professional indifference. Her parents' faith and perseverance became a quiet indictment of a nation's unequal grief.

When scholars later wrote about "representation in disappearance," Phoenix's name appeared beside cases like Tamika Huston, Mitrice Richardson, and others whose stories illuminated racial gaps in justice.

The Coldons never sought fame — only fairness.

And through their persistence, they gave voice to an entire movement that now refuses to let missing Black women be forgotten again.

CHAPTER 5 THEORIES AND TRUTHS

By the time three years had passed without a single confirmed sighting, Phoenix Coldon's name had become more question than memory. For her parents, the search was no longer just about *where* she went — it was about *why*.

Some nights, Goldia found herself replaying that final Sunday like a movie, pausing each moment to ask, *What did I miss?*

Did Phoenix plan her departure?

Was she taken?

Or was something darker at work — something that couldn't be explained by logic or chance?

Every theory seemed possible. Every answer led to another wound.

The Runaway Theory

The first and most persistent explanation offered by police was that Phoenix had left voluntarily — that she'd walked away from her life, overwhelmed by expectations, craving independence.

On paper, it sounded plausible. She was a young adult living at home, straddling the space between childhood and autonomy. Friends said she'd been restless. Some mentioned she'd spoken of wanting "a new start."

Investigators pointed to a private Facebook account discovered months later under an alias — "Monique Allen." On that page, Phoenix had shared cryptic posts about freedom, frustration, and faith. Some messages hinted at emotional conflict, others at a secret life she hadn't shared with her parents.

To some, it was proof she wanted out.

But to her mother, it was heartbreakingly incomplete.

"People write things when they're searching," Goldia said. "It doesn't mean they don't love their life. It means they're trying to understand it."

Moreover, the logistics didn't fit.

Phoenix left without her glasses, purse, ID, or money. Her car was found running in the middle of the road — hardly the action of someone executing a plan. And if she'd started a new life, how had she managed to stay invisible in a world wired with cameras, credit trails, and DNA databases?

There were no withdrawals from her accounts. No social security activity. No confirmed sightings.

If she ran away, she vanished more perfectly than most fugitives could.

The Abduction Theory

The second possibility was abduction.

The way her SUV was found — engine running, driver's door open — suggested interruption. Investigators considered the chance that she had been approached while stopped, perhaps forced out at gunpoint or lured by someone she trusted.

Old Jamestown Road, though suburban, bordered patches of undeveloped land and was lightly trafficked on Sundays. It was a place where someone could disappear without immediate notice.

But there were no screams reported, no tire marks suggesting a chase or struggle. Witnesses who drove that route that day remembered nothing unusual — no confrontation, no car following hers.

Still, both Goldia and Lawrence believed abduction was the most logical explanation. They suspected someone she knew might have coerced her — someone who understood her trust, her faith, and her obedience to authority.

"Phoenix wouldn't have just walked away," Lawrence said. "She was cautious. She knew right from wrong. If she left that car, it's because she thought she'd be right back — or because she had no choice."

The possibility of human trafficking, though terrifying, couldn't be ignored.

The Trafficking Theory

In the years after Phoenix vanished, multiple reports emerged of women abducted near Missouri interstates and funneled through trafficking networks operating across the Midwest. St. Louis, located near I-70 and I-44, had become a known hub for such activity — with truck stops and motels serving as frequent intersections between predators and victims.

The Coldons' private investigator pursued leads that suggested Phoenix might have been forced into such a network. One tip claimed she'd been seen in Illinois. Another suggested Texas. None were ever verified, but the pattern was enough to haunt her family.

Goldia began reading survivor accounts — stories of women taken, renamed, moved from city to city, stripped of their identities until they no longer recognized themselves. Some were found years later, their lives fragmented but intact.

The idea that Phoenix might still be alive — enslaved, hidden, unable to speak — was unbearable, yet it offered something that complete despair could not: *possibility*.

"I pray she's somewhere she can still call out to God," Goldia said quietly. "Because if she can, then she's still my daughter, and there's still hope."

The Mental Health Theory

A fourth theory emerged quietly, whispered rather than announced — that Phoenix might have been struggling with mental or emotional distress.

In the weeks before she vanished, her friends described her as contemplative, withdrawn. Some said she spoke about "feeling trapped," about wanting "something different." To a few confidantes, she hinted at pressure — the weight of expectations, the tension between faith and freedom.

Her parents' strict household, while rooted in love, may have amplified her desire for autonomy. She was expected to live by Biblical principles, remain home until marriage, and maintain a certain image within their church. That kind of environment, some said, could make anyone feel torn.

But while emotional strain might explain conflict, it didn't explain the disappearance's logistics — the running car, the silent phone, the total absence of trace. Depression does not erase footprints.

Still, for her family, even the mention of mental instability felt like an erasure — an attempt to explain away rather than understand.

"They wanted to make her a stereotype," Goldia once told a journalist. "Either the angry young woman or the fragile one. Phoenix was neither. She was simply human — with questions, dreams, and a mind too deep for easy labels."

The Theory That Remains

More than a decade later, no single theory satisfies all the facts. The truth about what happened to Phoenix Coldon lives in the uneasy space between them — where choice and coercion blur, where faith meets fear.

The official case remains open but inactive. Each year, on December 18th, her parents hold a candlelight vigil near Old Jamestown Road. They pray for answers, but also for others — for the unseen, the unheard, the unnamed.

They have learned that truth does not always arrive as a revelation. Sometimes, it arrives as endurance.

Goldia once said:

"People think hope is something you feel. It's not. Hope is something you *do*. Every time I say my daughter's name, that's hope."

And so, they keep saying it.

Phoenix.

A name that refuses to fade — a name that means rebirth.

CHAPTER 6 A MOTHER'S FAITH, A FATHER'S SILENCE

For the Coldons, grief did not come as a flood.

It came as a drought — a slow, relentless absence that dried up laughter, routine, and sleep. It seeped into every corner of their home, into every prayer, into every unanswered ring of the phone.

A missing child changes time.

Days stop being days; they become cycles of waiting. The Coldons' house, once filled with music and chatter, now pulsed with quiet desperation — the television tuned low in case the phone rang, the blinds half-closed against the pity of neighbors.

Goldia prayed out loud every morning. Lawrence barely spoke.

Two Languages of Grief

Where Goldia's pain was sound, Lawrence's was silence.

She filled the air with action — organizing, posting, calling, searching. She refused to let stillness take root. Her faith was kinetic; she moved because to stop was to drown.

He, on the other hand, folded inward. A former Air Force officer and man of quiet resolve, Lawrence had always been the steady one. But after Phoenix disappeared, steadiness became isolation. He spent hours in the garage, fixing things that didn't need repair — the lawnmower, the fence, the locks on the shed. Anything that gave him the illusion of control.

When Goldia wept, Lawrence held her, but his own tears came only once — at the impound lot, the first time he saw the empty driver's seat. After that, he rarely spoke Phoenix's name aloud. Not because he'd given up, but because it hurt too much to hear it echo back.

"He loves her in silence," Goldia once told a reporter.

"That's his way of praying."

Faith Under Fire

Before Phoenix's disappearance, the Coldons were known in their church as a family of unshakable faith. They attended services twice a week, volunteered in youth ministry, and treated Scripture as compass and comfort. But after that December day, even the most familiar verses felt foreign.

"Trust in the Lord with all your heart…"

The words sounded different when your daughter was gone and heaven refused to answer.

Goldia wrestled with her belief the way Jacob wrestled with the angel — clinging, demanding a blessing even in pain. She quoted Psalms through tears, read Job by lamplight, and filled her journals with both gratitude and fury.

"I love You, Lord," she wrote once.

"But I need to see Your mercy with my eyes."

She began to find a strange kind of clarity in her anger — not a loss of faith, but a breaking open of it.

Faith, she realized, wasn't a guarantee of comfort. It was a call to stand in darkness without running away.

The Marriage That Changed

The disappearance didn't just take their daughter; it reshaped their marriage.

Before, they had been partners in rhythm — predictable, reliable, strong. After, they became two grieving planets orbiting the same loss from different directions.

Goldia chased visibility, speaking publicly about Phoenix's case, appearing on talk shows, joining advocacy panels. Lawrence avoided cameras. The spotlight felt like an invasion of something sacred.

When reporters came to their home, he would quietly step out to the backyard. There, among the fading rose bushes, he prayed in whispers too low for microphones.

For months, they slept in separate rooms — not out of anger, but exhaustion. Each found solace in their own rituals. She wrote letters to her missing daughter. He built things with his hands — small birdhouses, crosses, shelves — physical prayers in the language of wood and nails.

It took years before they learned how to grieve together again.

Their love didn't vanish; it evolved. It became quieter, heavier, but still rooted in the same soil — faith, duty, and the shared belief that love is not erased by distance.

The Church and the Questions

Their church community rallied at first — organizing prayer vigils, raising awareness, delivering meals. But as time went on, attendance at those vigils thinned. The world has a short attention span for other people's pain.

Some church members offered well-meaning platitudes that stung: *"She's in a better place."*

Others implied she must have done something to end up in danger.

Each comment deepened Goldia's realization that faith communities are not immune to bias or fatigue.

She eventually found solace in smaller gatherings — quiet prayer circles of mothers who understood the unique ache of not knowing. Women who had buried children envied her uncertainty; she envied their closure.

Together, they learned how to live between hope and grief, how to call out to a God who sometimes stays silent, yet somehow still present.

The Unseen Cost

Behind the public face of strength lay private cracks. Financially, the Coldons drained their savings on private investigators and travel expenses. Lawrence cut back on work hours to stay available for searches. Goldia's health began to falter — sleepless nights, high blood pressure, panic episodes that came without warning.

There were days when she couldn't bring herself to leave the house. She'd sit on Phoenix's bed, touching the pillowcase like it could transmit memory.

"It still smells like her," she told a documentary crew once. "I wash everything in this house except that."

Yet even in her lowest moments, she refused despair the final word.

"Every day without my daughter is a battle," she said. "But faith doesn't always feel like light. Sometimes faith is just not giving up."

Love That Endures

Over the years, the Coldons' search transformed from an act of desperation into a ministry of endurance. They began speaking at schools and churches about faith, justice, and visibility. Their story became a vessel for others — parents searching for missing children, families fighting silence, communities learning empathy.

People often asked Goldia how she could keep believing after so many years without answers. Her reply was always the same:

"Because love doesn't end when a body disappears. Love is eternal, just like the soul. So I will keep loving my daughter until we meet again — whether in this life or the next."

Lawrence never said much at those events, but when he stood beside her, the quiet strength in his eyes said everything words could not.

In the end, their faith didn't bring the miracle they prayed for — not yet. But it carried them through the years when miracles seemed impossible.

And that, perhaps, was miracle enough.

CHAPTER 7 THE ECHO IN THE WIRES

The search for Phoenix did not end; it changed address.

What wouldn't surface in press briefings or nightly news began to bloom in podcasts, subreddits, Facebook groups, and late-night message boards where strangers traded theories the way old detectives once swapped notes at diners. The analog silence that had starved the case for years gave way to a digital chorus—sometimes brilliant, sometimes reckless, always loud.

It started slowly. A true-crime podcast devoted an hour to Phoenix's story, and downloads spiked. The host favored empathy over spectacle, repeating her name often, pausing long enough for listeners to feel the weight of a car idling on a winter road. After the episode, the inbox filled: a classmate remembered a comment from campus; a clerk thought she recognized Phoenix from a store weeks earlier; a neighbor recalled a dark SUV parked on Old Jamestown more than once. None of it solved anything, but all of it proved a point—memory needs invitation.

Soon, YouTube essays followed—some carefully sourced, others stitched together from rumor and a confident voiceover. A small army of amateur sleuths drew maps, traced timelines, and overlaid them with pins and arrows. The effect was both inspiring and unnerving. Where official files were thin, the internet tried to thicken them with inference.

The Crowd That Helps—and Hurts

Crowd-sourcing brought good work. A volunteer geospatial analyst modeled sightlines along Old Jamestown and identified blind corners where a person could be moved out of view in seconds. A data-savvy listener filed public-records requests that turned up a small cache of unreviewed tips. A young attorney offered pro-bono help to clarify jurisdictional confusion from the first week.

But the same current carried debris. One forum misidentified a man in Phoenix's social circle, and within hours his employer received angry emails. A content creator declared trafficking "definitive" based on a single unverified sighting. Another suggested Phoenix had engineered a new life and scolded the family for not accepting it. Doxing demands masqueraded as justice; suspicion became a hobby with casualties.

Goldia and Lawrence watched it all with a mix of gratitude and dread. The internet could multiply their daughter's reach, but it could also turn her into a commodity—another unsolved tale to be optimized for clicks. They learned, painfully, that attention and care are not the same thing.

The Case File in the Cloud

Digital revival nudged the official case. When a documentary revisited the disappearance, the county tip line saw a short surge. Investigators re-interviewed two witnesses who—after hearing their own words a decade later—remembered more than they had said the first time. A traffic camera once thought irrelevant was located in an archival server; its footage window missed Phoenix's car by minutes, but its metadata narrowed the timeline by ten.

Not all leads aged well. A "new sighting" in another state turned out to be a woman with similar features, mortified by the sudden attention. A voicemail promising "the truth" dissolved into a request for money. Still, amid the false starts were small verifications—little stones that, arranged carefully, could edge a path forward.

Ethics in a Digital Storm

Podcast hosts learned to include disclaimers about speculation, and moderators wrote house rules: no naming uncharged persons, no gossip about mental health, no posting unverified addresses. The best creators began inviting experts—behavioral analysts, missing-persons advocates, trauma counselors—to explain how memory works, why investigations stall, and how families survive the long middle. They reminded audiences that a mystery is not a playground; it is someone's life.

When they reached out, the Coldons said yes selectively. They preferred the interviewers who did their homework, who asked permission before airing private photos, who understood that sorrow has a metabolism and cannot be sped up for broadcast. On camera, Goldia held a balance that impressed even skeptics: open enough to help, guarded enough to protect a daughter who could not speak for herself.

Digital Footprints, Human Steps

The most practical gains came from quiet corners: a volunteer spreadsheet that centralized known tips; a shared folder of mapped search zones; a rotating schedule of social posts timed for maximum visibility in the cities most likely to matter. A small nonprofit taught the Coldons how to run geo-targeted flyers and how to archive every message for chain-of-custody if a tip ever reached court.

One evening, months into the renewed attention, an email arrived from a woman who had left a controlling relationship years earlier. She said Phoenix's story felt familiar—the quick step out of a car, the promise to "be right back." She described methods abusers use to separate victims from phones and ID, to keep them close while making them untraceable. It wasn't a confession or a lead; it was a lens. Sometimes the most important tip is a way of seeing.

The Afterlife of a Mystery

The internet does not do endings. It loops. Each re-tell becomes a new beginning for someone who has never heard the story. A fresh thumbnail, a reposted thread, a curated "timeline explained" video: the case persists, both preserved and distorted by repetition.

For the Coldons, the echo carried a paradox. Visibility meant hope —more eyes, more chances, more serendipity. But it also meant reliving Day One, again and again, for audiences that would move on to the next upload by morning. They learned to set boundaries, to log off when speculation turned cruel, to measure progress not by viral arcs but by the steady accumulation of good work: a new contact at an agency, a reopened file, a stranger who now knew Phoenix's name.

On the anniversary each year, a wave of posts appears: candles, prayers, maps, clips of Goldia's voice. Some are performative, yes. Many are not. In the quiet after the spike, the family returns to their ritual—coffee, prayer, emails, the long faithful labor of waiting. Offline, the house is still. The chair by the window is still. The road outside is the same road as always, ordinary and terrible in its indifference.

What the Wires Can—and Can't—Do

The echo in the wires has given Phoenix something the first years denied her: sustained attention, a community of care, and occasional movement where there was once none. It has also taught a harder truth: technology can amplify a search, but it cannot redeem an investigation that never received the care it deserved. Only people can do that—people with badges and budgets, people with microphones and ethics, people who remember that a case file is a life.

If the internet has a blessing to offer, it is this: a place where strangers can become witnesses, and where a name can keep being said long after official interest fades. It is imperfect and unruly. It is also, sometimes, enough to keep a candle lit on a windowsill that refuses to darken.

And so the echo continues—packets of hope traveling the same wires as rumor, a mother scrolling past the noise to find the one message that might matter, a father watching from the doorway as the screen light touches his wife's face. Somewhere, a tab stays open. Somewhere, a cursor blinks like a heartbeat. Somewhere, a story refuses the quiet.

CHAPTER 8 THE SEARCHES

The map of Missouri, once a familiar outline, had become something else entirely for the Coldons. It was no longer just geography — it was testimony. Each red mark was a rumor followed, each circle a day spent walking fields, knocking on doors, listening to silence.

By 2014, Phoenix had been missing nearly three years.

In that time, Goldia and Lawrence had traveled more miles than they could count. Their car's odometer climbed like a calendar. They carried stacks of flyers everywhere — the same photo: Phoenix smiling, radiant, unaware that this image would become her public face.

Every lead mattered. Every call could be *the* one.

And yet, most weren't.

The Girl in Texas

The first call that felt credible came from Houston. A woman named Carla said she'd seen someone who looked exactly like Phoenix — same height, same smile, even the same dimple when she laughed. She worked at a women's shelter and had noticed a newcomer who kept to herself, refused to share her name, and prayed alone every night.

Goldia's heart leapt. She wrote down every detail. Lawrence called their private investigator, and within forty-eight hours, he was on a flight to Texas. The shelter's director met him in the parking lot.

"We thought it might be her," the director said softly, "but the woman left two nights ago."

Security footage was grainy. The girl on screen did look like Phoenix — the walk, the posture, even the way she tucked her hair behind her ear. But when they enhanced the image, the resemblance fractured. It wasn't her.

The investigator called Goldia from the road. She didn't cry. She simply said, "Then we keep looking."

That was her refrain — always the same, steady, defiant.

The Call from Illinois

Months later, another lead.

This time from a gas station attendant in East St. Louis who swore he'd seen Phoenix pumping gas late one night, alone. He remembered her because she seemed nervous, glancing over her shoulder as if someone was watching.

The police followed up, but surveillance footage had already been recorded over. The attendant's memory became the only evidence, and even that began to blur under questioning. Was the date right? Could he describe the car?

"I remember her," he said, hesitating. "But maybe it was someone else."

For families of the missing, hope is both medicine and poison. It heals just enough to make survival possible, then breaks the heart all over again.

The Private Investigator

The Coldons eventually hired **C.J. Corder**, a retired detective known for taking cases the system had abandoned. He was direct, pragmatic, and unafraid to challenge police. His first observation was blunt:

"They should've treated this as a crime scene from the beginning. By now, we're working with dust."

Corder reviewed every document, every tip, every rumor. He drove Old Jamestown Road repeatedly, stopping at each bend and shoulder.

His theory leaned toward abduction — likely someone Phoenix knew. "That car didn't end up there by accident," he said. "She was stopped. She trusted whoever made her stop."

He also explored the trafficking angle, tracing reports of women moved between Missouri and Kansas City. None led to Phoenix, but they revealed something darker — a pattern that made her case both singular and systemic.

He stayed in touch with the family for years, long after funding ran out. "You don't walk away from people like the Coldons," he told a journalist later. "They make you remember why you started doing this in the first place."

The Tip That Shattered Hope

In 2016, a tip arrived from a man claiming to have information about Phoenix's whereabouts — but he wanted money. He said she was alive, living under another name in Atlanta.

The Coldons debated for days whether to respond. Desperation erodes caution. In the end, they sent the contact to law enforcement. The man vanished as quickly as he had appeared.

Weeks later, investigators traced the number to a scammer who had targeted other missing-person families.

Goldia was inconsolable.

"How can someone use a mother's pain for profit?" she asked.

It wasn't a question anyone could answer.

The Small Mercies

Between the false starts came moments that didn't advance the case but sustained the spirit.

At one church event, a young woman approached Goldia in tears. "Your daughter's story saved me," she said. "I was about to give up on my family, but I saw how hard you fight for yours. I called my mother again."

Goldia hugged her. Later that night, she told Lawrence, "Even if we never find Phoenix, her story is saving people."

Another mercy came in the form of a letter — handwritten, anonymous. It contained no clues, only compassion:

"You do not know me, but I pray for your daughter every morning at sunrise. She is not forgotten."

It was postmarked from Denver. They never learned who sent it, but Goldia kept it taped inside her Bible. The ink faded over time, but the message remained bright.

The Weight of Hope

Each passing year forced the Coldons to reinvent hope. At first, it was *find her*. Then it became *find answers*. Eventually, it settled into *find peace*.

The vigils continued, candles flickering against December wind. The same prayers, the same faces, the same hollow in the air where

Phoenix's laughter used to be.

Goldia began to speak less about outcomes and more about meaning.

"People think faith means believing she's alive," she said. "But sometimes faith means believing that even this — this pain — will be used for good somehow."

Lawrence, still quiet, had his own ritual. Every Sunday evening, he drove alone down Old Jamestown Road, parking for a few minutes near where her car was found. He didn't talk or pray aloud. He just sat.

"It's where I feel closest to her," he told a friend once. "The world stopped there for her. Maybe it'll start again for me."

The Long View

By 2018, most cold cases from 2011 had already been archived. But Phoenix's file remained open, if only because her parents refused to let it close. They kept sending new information to the FBI and kept pushing for DNA comparisons when unidentified remains surfaced anywhere near Missouri. Each time, they waited for results with the same uneasy hope — a paradoxical wish both for and against closure.

When none matched, Goldia whispered thanks and sorrow in the same breath.

The not-knowing was torture, but finality might have been worse.

And so they continued, one lead at a time, one prayer at a time.

Because for the Coldons, even a false start was better than no start at all.

And every mercy — no matter how small — was a sign that love still reached across the silence.

CHAPTER 9
UNFINISHED
ANSWERS

There is a peculiar ache in not knowing. It doesn't fade — it adapts.

For **Goldia and Lawrence Coldon**, uncertainty became a second language, one they learned to live inside without letting it consume them.

By the tenth year of Phoenix's disappearance, their search had evolved into something larger than a personal crusade. It became a movement — quiet but enduring — for visibility, equality, and compassion in a system that too often measures whose stories are worth pursuing.

And yet, after all the vigils, interviews, and prayers, one truth remained: **there were still no answers.**

The Case That Changed Conversations

Phoenix's case began as one family's tragedy. But it became a lens — exposing cracks in how America tells stories about missing people.

Before 2011, few national databases included race as a searchable category. Few journalists questioned why some faces received wall-to-wall coverage while others barely flickered across screens. The Coldons didn't set out to start a conversation about bias; they simply wanted their daughter found. But in doing so, they forced a reckoning.

Advocacy groups began citing her case in lectures and reports. **The Black and Missing Foundation** used Phoenix's story to illustrate how delays in coverage often lead to irreversible investigative gaps. **Faith-based networks** invited Goldia to speak about the intersection of race, faith, and perseverance.

In a 2020 symposium on systemic disparities, a sociologist remarked:

"Phoenix Coldon's name lives where policy meets prayer — a reminder that visibility is not charity, it's justice."

Seeds of Change

From that reckoning grew tangible action. Missouri law enforcement introduced updated training modules on handling missing-person cases, emphasizing early interagency coordination and media engagement — the very failures that had plagued Phoenix's investigation.

Churches across St. Louis began hosting quarterly awareness drives, teaching families how to file reports quickly and protect digital footprints.

And the Coldons, unwilling to let their pain be wasted, co-founded a small nonprofit: **The Phoenix Initiative** — a name chosen not just for their daughter, but for what she represented. The group provided support for families navigating missing-person bureaucracy, offering prayer, paperwork help, and emotional counseling.

They couldn't resurrect answers, but they could light the path for others still searching.

"If we can save one family from feeling alone," Goldia said, "then some part of our pain has done its job."

Faith Reimagined

A decade of waiting transforms belief. The Coldons' faith no longer fit the simple categories of miracle and mystery. It had matured into something steadier — faith as endurance, faith as stewardship.

For Goldia, that meant letting go of bargaining prayers — the "if You bring her back, I'll…" kind. Instead, her faith became about meaning.

"Maybe we were chosen for this," she told a women's retreat in 2019. "Not as punishment, but as purpose."

Lawrence's faith took a quieter form. He still drove Old Jamestown Road on Sunday evenings. Sometimes, he left a single flower at the roadside. He never explained why. He didn't have to. Faith, for him, wasn't words — it was showing up.

The Broader Lesson

Phoenix's story is about more than one disappearance. It's about the hierarchy of attention — how justice itself can depend on whose pain fits the narrative.

Her absence revealed the need for new systems, new ethics, and new empathy. It exposed the moral cost of selective visibility.

And it reminded the world that missing-person cases don't end when the news cameras leave; they end when the families are finally allowed to stop searching — and sometimes, that moment never comes.

The Echo of Her Name

Each year, when December 18th comes around, hundreds gather for a vigil in St. Louis. They light candles, sing hymns, and speak names — not just Phoenix's, but those of other missing daughters, sons, and friends.

The crowd always falls silent when Goldia takes the microphone. Her voice carries the cadence of both preacher and mother.

"We are not here for closure," she tells them. "We are here for continuation — for the belief that love still has work to do."

Somewhere in that crowd, faces glisten in candlelight — strangers united by loss, and by the quiet recognition that to remember is a form of resistance.

As the choir hums the final verse of *Amazing Grace*, Goldia looks up. The night sky above St. Louis is clear, dotted with stars. Somewhere, she imagines, her daughter is seeing the same sky.

And that thought — fragile, unprovable, luminous — is enough to keep her standing.

The Meaning of "Unfinished"

For most people, the word *unfinished* implies failure. But for the Coldons, it became sacred. It meant the story wasn't over, the hope wasn't extinguished, and love hadn't run out of places to go.

The police may still call it an open case. The world may have moved on. But for those who speak Phoenix's name, the investigation is not just about evidence — it's about empathy, equity, and the enduring power of one family's refusal to stop believing.

In that sense, Phoenix's story *is* rebirth — the meaning of her name fulfilled.

Out of silence came advocacy. Out of pain came purpose.

And out of darkness came a light that refuses to go out.

EPILOGUE

— *The Light That Stayed*

The seasons kept changing, as they always do.

The house on the quiet St. Louis street still stands, its windows dressed with the same curtains Phoenix once helped her mother hem. Her trophies line the hallway shelf, dusted carefully every Sunday. Her Bible remains on her bedside table, open to the same verse her parents read aloud the night before she vanished:

"For we walk by faith, not by sight." — *2 Corinthians 5:7*

At first, those words felt cruel — a reminder of all they could not see, all they had lost. But over time, they became an anchor. Faith, they discovered, was not certainty. It was endurance. It was choosing to believe that light still matters, even when it doesn't lead you home.

Each December, the Coldons light a single candle in their front window. It's not for the press, not for the neighbors, not even for closure. It's for Phoenix — and for every parent who keeps searching.

The flame burns through the night, small but steady, casting just enough glow to be seen from the road. Sometimes, cars slow as they pass, and someone honks softly — a signal that they remember.

The Living Legacy

In the years since, *The Phoenix Initiative* has grown quietly. They've helped dozens of families fill out missing-person paperwork, coordinate with detectives, and cope with the numbing bureaucracy of grief. The Coldons' phone rings less often with tips about Phoenix and more with calls that begin, "Can you help us?"

And always, they do.

"We can't find everyone," Goldia says, "but we can make sure no one feels invisible."

Their living room has become a sanctuary — half office, half prayer room. Bulletin boards hold photos of other missing sons and daughters. Some have been found. Others remain shadows. But each is spoken aloud during morning devotions, their names rising like incense.

The Silence That Speaks

Some nights, when the house is quiet, Goldia walks to Phoenix's room and sits on the edge of the bed. She traces her fingers along the comforter, whispers a prayer, and imagines her daughter's laughter echoing faintly through the air.

"I don't talk to her spirit," she once told a reporter. "I talk to God about her. He's the only one who can reach that far."

There's no bitterness in her voice anymore — only calm. Grief has been transformed into ministry, absence into calling.

Lawrence still drives Old Jamestown Road on anniversaries. The shoulder where Phoenix's car was found is now overgrown with grass, but he knows exactly where to stop. He rolls down the window and listens — to the wind, to memory, to something beyond both.

"People think the story ended there," he says quietly. "But I think that's where it began."

The World Moves On

Time has a way of thinning headlines.

New stories rise, new tragedies claim the cycle. But in the small circles where faith and perseverance meet, Phoenix's name still travels. Her story is told in classrooms, church pulpits, and advocacy conferences.

It's no longer just about a missing girl. It's about what she revealed — the unseen, the uncounted, the unsearched.

Every retelling becomes a prayer disguised as a narrative: *Remember her. Remember them. Remember to care.*

The Light That Stayed

The Coldons have stopped asking *why*. That question, they learned, only deepens the wound. Instead, they ask *how*:

How can we make this pain serve others? How can we keep her light alive? How can we walk by faith, not by sight?

In that shift lies survival — and redemption.

The night Phoenix disappeared, a single car idled by the side of the road. No witnesses. No clear answers. Only questions. But from that silence, something extraordinary rose — a faith that refused to fade, a movement born of grief, and a family that turned absence into action.

And in the flicker of one candle on a quiet December night, that faith still burns — not as an ending, but as an invitation:

To see.

To search.

To believe that even in the deepest darkness, there is a light that stays.

A PERSONAL REQUEST

Thank you for reading *Runaway or Taken? The Mystery of Phoenix Coldon.*

If this book resonated with you, I'd be deeply grateful if you left a written review. Even tapping a star rating—without writing anything—helps more than you might realize. It signals to bookstores and platforms that this story matters.

To leave a review, please visit the Amazon page:

Runaway or Taken? : The Mystery of Phoenix Coldon

[replace with your book's Amazon review link]

Or scan the QR code in this section to go directly to the review page.

Your support helps ensure Phoenix Coldon's story—and others like it—are not forgotten.

With gratitude,

Linda Davidson

ABOUT THE AUTHOR

Linda Davidson is a writer of true crime and historical nonfiction dedicated to uncovering the stories that live in the shadows of history. Her work focuses on untold narratives, unsolved mysteries, and the profound human cost behind the headlines that often reduce victims to statistics. With a background in research and a passion for justice, she approaches each case with empathy, care, and relentless curiosity.

Rather than glorifying criminals, Linda's mission is to restore dignity to the lives cut short and to highlight the resilience of families and communities who continue to seek answers. Her writing blends meticulous research with vivid, compelling storytelling, drawing readers into the emotional and cultural contexts of each case while honoring the victims at its center.

When she is not writing, Linda studies criminal psychology, follows ongoing investigations, and supports awareness efforts for missing persons and unsolved crimes. She believes that true crime, when told responsibly, can shine a light on systemic failures, honor those who can no longer speak for themselves, and remind us that justice—though sometimes delayed or denied—remains worth pursuing.

ALSO BY THE LINDA DAVIDSON

TIMELINE (CONDENSED)

- **May 23, 1988** — Birth of Phoenix Reeves Coldon, St. Louis, MO.
- **Dec 18, 2011** — Vehicle found on Old Jamestown Road; Phoenix reported missing.
- **2012–2014** — Community searches; jurisdiction clarification; media outreach.
- **2013** — National TV feature brings broader attention.
- **2015–2020** — Continued advocacy; case remains open.
- **2021–Present** — Digital revivals; nonprofit support to other families.

SUPPORT RESOURCES FOR FAMILIES OF THE MISSING

If someone is missing right now

- **Call 911** and file a report immediately (adults and minors). There is **no waiting period** in the U.S.
- Ask for the case number and the lead investigator's name/phone.
- Preserve evidence: **don't** clean the person's room/car/devices. Note last known clothing, medications, vehicle plate/VIN, and recent photos.
- Identify one family **point of contact** to coordinate with law enforcement and media.

National hotlines & case support (U.S.)

- **988 Suicide & Crisis Lifeline** — 988 (24/7 text/call/chat)
- **National Human Trafficking Hotline (Polaris)** — 1-888-373-7888 or text *233733*
- **RAINN (sexual assault support)** — 1-800-656-HOPE
- **NAMI HelpLine (mental health)** — 1-800-950-NAMI (Mon–Fri) or text *HELPLINE* to 62640
- **National Runaway Safeline** — 1-800-RUNAWAY (youth, parents)
- **Eldercare Locator** — 1-800-677-1116 (adults with cognitive impairment)

Missing-person case infrastructure (U.S.)

- **NamUs (National Missing and Unidentified Persons System):** Public database for missing/unidentified cases; work with LE to create a profile and submit DNA/

dental/fingerprints.

- **NCMEC (National Center for Missing & Exploited Children):** For minors; poster creation, case support, Team Adam rapid response.
- **Black and Missing Foundation (BAMFI):** Awareness, case amplification, family liaison services.
- **DNA Doe Project / The Doe Network:** For unidentified remains and cold-case connections (usually via law enforcement).
- **Bureau of Indian Affairs, Missing & Murdered Unit (MMU):** For cases involving Native communities.
- **Texas EquuSearch / regional SAR nonprofits:** Trained volunteer searches (availability varies by region).

Practical steps & checklists

Family command basics

- Make a **master log** (date/time, who you spoke with, what was shared, next steps).
- Gather: recent **high-resolution photos**, medical/dental records, fingerprints (if available), device/vehicle info, known hangouts, friends, routines.
- Request: entry into **NCIC** (via police), **NamUs**, and for minors an **NCMEC poster**.
- Ask investigators about: phone records, license-plate reader hits, traffic/business cams, bank/credit activity, transit card data.

Digital safety & outreach

- Pin a public post with **verified facts**, case number, and tip line. Avoid unvetted rumors.
- Save screenshots of online tips; **don't** confront or dox anyone.
- Back up the missing person's accounts/devices through law enforcement or a forensic specialist before accessing.

Working with media

- Prepare a **one-page fact sheet**: name, age, last seen (date/time/place), clothing/vehicle, medical needs, official tip line, family contact.
- Share **one clear photo** (face forward, no filters).
- Repeat: "**All tips to [agency/number].**"

Search coordination

- Coordinate with law enforcement or a reputable SAR group.
- Provide maps, assign teams, use sign-in/out sheets, photograph notable findings in place, and log GPS tracks.
- **Do not** enter dangerous terrain or private property without permission.

Evidence & legal

- Request a **forensic exam** of the vehicle/room/devices before cleaning.
- Discuss **voluntary DNA** (family reference samples) for NamUs matching.
- Consider **power of attorney/financial holds** if an adult is missing long-term (consult an attorney).

Emotional & practical support

- **Homicide Survivors/Trauma centers** (city or county): free counseling and victim-services navigation.
- **Faith and community groups:** meals, childcare, search volunteers.
- **Support communities:** private peer groups for families of the missing can reduce isolation.

Templates (quick copy)

Public post (pin):

"**Missing Person**: [Full Name, Age]. Last seen [date/time] near [location], wearing [description]. Case #[####], agency: [Dept/

Detective, phone/email]. If you saw [Name] or have video (ring/dash/traffic) from [time window], **please call [official tip line]**. Do not post rumors—send tips directly to investigators."

Media email subject:

"Urgent: Missing [Age]-year-old from [City] — Case #[####], interview availability today"

Flyer essentials:

Recent face photo · Name/Age/Height/Weight · Last-seen details · Distinguishing features/medical needs · Case # & official tip line · QR to NamUs/NCMEC page.

For specific communities

- **Indigenous:** BIA MMU; Sovereign Bodies Institute; National Indigenous Women's Resource Center.
- **LGBTQ+: Trans Lifeline** (community support) — 877-565-8860.
- **College/University cases:** Campus police, Title IX office, student affairs, and local PD must coordinate; request a **timely warning** if criteria are met.
- **Dementia/Autism/IDD:** Ask police about **Silver Alert** eligibility; enroll in local **Safe Return/Project Lifesaver** programs.

International (quick starters)

- **UK:** Missing People — call/text **116 000** (free, 24/7).
- **Canada:** Missing Children Society of Canada; local police + **Crime Stoppers** (1-800-222-TIPS).
- **Australia:** National Missing Persons Coordination Centre (AFP); **Crime Stoppers** (1800 333 000).
- **EU:** Missing Children Europe — **116 000** across member states.

What to say when you need help

- "We need assistance creating a NamUs/NCMEC entry and coordinating a trained search."
- "Please confirm NCIC entry and provide our case

number and lead detective contact."

- "We request review of [date/time] traffic/business cameras within a 1–2 mile radius of [location]."

A NOTE TO READERS

If this book moved you, consider taking one specific action: share a current missing-person flier from your area, donate to a vetted advocacy group, or attend a local awareness event. Visibility isn't charity; it's a form of justice.

AUTHOR'S NOTE ON SOURCES & ETHICS

This narrative is built from publicly available materials: police and court records, broadcast transcripts, interview archives, documentary segments, advocacy reports, and first-person testimonies where consent was explicit. Where accounts conflict or records are incomplete, I identify uncertainty and avoid declaring motive or guilt. Composite scene-setting is used sparingly and only to convey place and process—not to invent facts. Direct quotes appear from recorded or published remarks. When time stamps or recollections diverge, the most conservative reading prevails.

Missing-persons cases involve living people and ongoing trauma. Identifying details of private individuals are limited or omitted where doing so adds protection without sacrificing clarity. The aim is simple: illuminate without exploiting.

HELP FIND PHOENIX COLDON

If you have *any* information—no matter how small—about the disappearance of **Phoenix Lucille Coldon**, please come forward.

Phoenix was last seen **on December 18, 2011**, leaving her family's home in **Spanish Lake, Missouri**. Her black 1998 Chevrolet Blazer was later found **abandoned in East St. Louis, Illinois**, with the keys still in the ignition and the engine running. Since that day, her family has lived with the ache of uncertainty—searching, praying, and refusing to give up.

Over a decade has passed, but *time does not erase truth*. A single recollection, message, or observation could be the missing piece that helps bring Phoenix home or finally answers what happened to her.

If you saw **Phoenix**, her **vehicle**, or **anything unusual** in the area of **9th Street and St. Clair Avenue** in East St. Louis on or around December 18, 2011—or if you have heard someone speak about the case with specific, unreported details—please reach out. Even information that seems insignificant could matter.

You can contact:

East St. Louis Police Department

☐ (618) 482-6727

Or, if you wish to remain anonymous:

CrimeStoppers St. Louis

☐ (866) 371-8477

www.stlrcs.org

You may also share information with the **National Center for Missing and Exploited Children (NCMEC)** at

 1-800-THE-LOST (1-800-843-5678).

If you prefer to communicate confidentially or off the record, please email:

phoenixcoldonproject@protonmail.com (for verified case advocates and researchers).

Every tip is reviewed and forwarded to the appropriate investigative team.

Phoenix Coldon was 23 years old when she disappeared. She deserves to be found.

Her family deserves answers.

And you may hold the key to truth.

If you know something—say something. Because silence helps no one.

ACKNOWLEDGMENTS

To the Coldon family—Goldia and Lawrence—thank you for your grace, courage, and perseverance. Your devotion to Phoenix, and to every family walking this hard road, set the moral compass for this book. You taught me what steadfast love looks like over years, not headlines.

To the advocates and caseworkers who labor in the quiet: community pastors and lay leaders; crisis-response teams; shelter staff; victim advocates; hotline responders; librarians who help pull records; and the volunteers who staple flyers in the rain, moderate forums responsibly, and show up when cameras don't. Your work is the spine of every search.

To investigators—current and retired—who shared procedures, limits, and lessons learned with candor; and to the journalists, producers, and podcasters who chose verification over virality. Your insistence on accuracy protected people who cannot protect themselves.

To early readers who kept me honest about language, dignity, and the difference between telling a story and guarding a life: thank you for the margin notes that began, "Be gentler here," and "Name only what you can source." You improved every chapter.

To legal and research friends who reviewed passages for fairness and clarity; to records clerks who guided me through request numbers and retention schedules; and to the NamUs and NGO staff who answered questions after hours—your patience widened the circle of truth.

To booksellers, librarians, teachers, and book-club hosts who make space for difficult conversations about justice and empathy: you help communities remember the missing by name.

To the readers who wrote with tips, corrections, or quiet encouragement; and to families who trusted me with pieces of your own stories—even when they did not belong in this book— your restraint and generosity shaped how I wrote what remained.

Finally, to Phoenix—whose absence continues to move people to care, to act, and to see: this book exists so your name is spoken with tenderness and resolve. May its pages help someone else feel less alone.

DISCUSSION QUESTIONS FOR BOOK CLUBS / CLASSROOMS

1. How can communities support families during the "long middle" after headlines fade?
2. Where is the line between public interest and exploitation in true-crime storytelling?
3. How do race and class shape the urgency of coverage and investigation?
4. Which theory in Phoenix's case seemed most persuasive to you—and why? What evidence would change your mind?
5. What practical steps can colleges, churches, and local organizations take to prevent disappearances and improve early response?

REFERENCES

- Black and Missing Foundation. (n.d.). *About us.* https://blackandmissinginc.com
- Council of Europe. (2017). *Information disorder: Toward an interdisciplinary framework for research and policy making* (Report by C. Wardle & H. Derakhshan). https://rm.coe.int/information-disorder-toward-an-interdisciplinary-framework-for-researc/168076277c
- Doe Network. (n.d.). *International center for unidentified & missing persons.* https://www.doenetwork.org
- Fisher, B. A. J., & Fisher, D. R. (2022). *Techniques of crime scene investigation* (10th ed.). CRC Press.
- National Center for Missing & Exploited Children. (n.d.). *Facts & stats.* https://www.missingkids.org/footer/media/keyfacts
- National Human Trafficking Hotline (Polaris). (n.d.). *Get help.* https://humantraffickinghotline.org
- National Institute of Justice. (2014). *Identifying the missing using DNA: A guide for families.* U.S. Department of Justice. https://nij.ojp.gov/library/publications/identifying-missing-using-dna-guide-families
- National Missing and Unidentified Persons System (NamUs). (n.d.). *NamUs—Official site.* https://namus.nij.ojp.gov
- Office for Victims of Crime. (2019). *When your child is missing: A family survival guide* (5th ed.). U.S. Department of Justice. https://ovc.ojp.gov/library/publications/when-

your-child-missing-family-survival-guide

- Texas Search and Rescue. (n.d.). *About TEXSAR*. https://www.texsar.org
- Worthington, E. L., Jr. (2006). *Forgiveness and reconciliation: Theory and application*. Routledge.

Media/ethics context

- Jones, S. (2009). *Trauma and grace: Theology in a ruptured world*. Westminster John Knox Press.
- Wardle, C., & Derakhshan, H. (2017). *Information disorder: Definitions, types, and solutions*. In *Information disorder* (pp. 17–68). Council of Europe. https://rm.coe.int/information-disorder-toward-an-interdisciplinary-framework-for-researc/168076277c

Printed in Dunstable, United Kingdom

79784342R00057